S0-BCJ-610

Mah Jong,
Anyone?

Mah Jong, Anyone?

A Manual of Western Play

REVISED EDITION

Kitty Strauser • Lucille Evans
with new material by Tom Sloper

TUTTLE PUBLISHING
Tokyo • Rutland, Vermont • Singapore

DEER PARK PUBLIC LIBRARY
44 LAKE AVENUE
DEER PARK, N.Y. 11729

First published in 2006 by Tuttle Publishing, an imprint of Periplus Editions (HK) Ltd., with editorial offices at 364 Innovation Drive, North Clarendon, Vermont 05759

Text copyright and illustrations copyright © 1964, 2006 Tuttle Publishing
All rights reserved. No part of this publication may be reproduced or utilized in any form or by any means, electronic or mechanical, including photocopying, recording, or by any information storage and retrieval system, without prior written permission from the publisher.

Library of Congress Cataloging-in-Publication Data

Strauser, Kitty.
  Mah jong, anyone? : a manual of western play / Kitty Strauser, Lucille Evans with new material by Tom Sloper.—Rev. ed.
    p. cm.
  Includes bibliographical references and index.
  ISBN 0-8048-3761-9 (pbk. : alk. paper)
1. Mah jong. I. Evans, Lucille, 1909- II. Sloper, Tom. III. Title.
GV1299.M3S78 2006
795.3'4--dc22
                    2006001127
ISBN-10: 0-8048-3761-9
ISBN-13: 978-0-8048-3761-3

Distributed by

North America, Latin America & Europe
Tuttle Publishing
364 Innovation Drive, North Clarendon,
VT 05759-9436
Tel: (802) 773-8930; Fax: (802) 773-6993
Email: info@tuttlepublishing.com
www.tuttlepublishing.com

Japan
Tuttle Publishing
Yaekari Building, 3rd Floor, 5-4-12 Osaki,
Shinagawa-ku, Tokyo 141 0032
Tel: (03) 5437-0171; Fax: (03) 5437-0755
Email: tuttle-sales@gol.com

Asia Pacific
Berkeley Books Pte. Ltd.
130 Joo Seng Road, #06-01
Singapore 368357
Tel: (65) 6280-1330; Fax: (65) 6280-6290
Email: inquiries@periplus.com.sg
www.periplus.com

Indonesia
PT Java Books Indonesia
Kawasan Industri Pulogadung
Jl. Rawa Gelam IV No. 9
Jakarta 13930 Indonesia
Tel: (021) 4682-1088; Fax: (021) 461-0207
Email: cs@javabooks.co.id

10 09 08 07 06   5 4 3 2 1

Printed in Singapore

TUTTLE PUBLISHING® is a registered trademark of Tuttle Publishing, a division of Periplus Editions (HK) Ltd.

Contents

Preface

You are a beginner and you have a Mah Jong set. Or perhaps you are thinking of buying one. In either case, this is your book, designed to help you know your set and to get the most enjoyment out of the game. If you are an old hand, you will find in this volume much of what you already know, simply stated and easily referenced, plus a comprehensive list of the most played special hands.

As Mah Jong fans for many years, we have played a wide range of systems and methods in the United States and many parts of the Far East. Based on our experience, observation, and study, three points stand out sharply:

1. Mah Jong, because of its basic simplicity and adaptability, is eternally appealing to all age groups. Initial curiosity is undoubtedly aroused by its exotic equipment, seemingly ritualistic methods of play, or possibly its ancient and curious origins and history, of which there are many versions. But its persistent popularity is due to its unlimited variety in play; its continuing development of fresh, new hands; and, most of all, the challenge of mastering these.

2. As skill and knowledge develop, it soon becomes apparent that there are almost as many ways to play aside from the original basic game as there are players.

3. There is a need for a concise description of the game most widely played in English-speaking countries, not only to instruct the

beginner, but also to serve as a reference for seasoned players. And that is the purpose of this manual.

For the sake of brevity we have omitted the history and background of Mah Jong and also descriptions of the numerous Asian variants because most Western players seem to prefer the excitement and stimulus of the wider-ranging adaptations that they themselves have brought to this absorbing game.

To claim completeness or ultimate authority in any field is to open the door to unending trouble. Therefore we point out that Chapters 1–4 of this manual represent a sincere attempt to set forth for beginners this modern method of playing Mah Jong and to give a detailed description of its equipment, terminology, rules, penalties, and scoring. In Chapter 5, for experienced players as well as novices, brief descriptions of the best-known special hands are listed. An entirely new section on strategy rounds out the book.

Mah Jong is primarily a game for four persons, and the instructions in this manual are given for that number. Two-, three-, five-, and six-handed games are possible although rarely played. However, two- and three-handed games are described briefly on pages 44–45.

You will inevitably discover new hands as soon as you start spending your days at Mah Jong. It is impossible to play Mah Jong without constantly learning something new, and that is the secret of its fascination.

Chapter 1
Equipment and Accessories

Western Mah Jong uses a set of 144 basic tiles. Extra tiles, if any, are not used in play. Accessories include four racks to hold the tiles while playing, counters to serve as money, dice, and a small container, such as a bowl, for the "kitty."

When buying a Mah Jong set be sure that suit and flower tiles are clearly marked with numbers and that the wind tiles are lettered.

A standard card table is suitable for playing but should be covered, if it is hard-surfaced, to reduce noise when shuffling the tiles.

If you are a beginner, spread your set out as you read the following.

Tiles

Tiles, usually made of plastic, bone, bamboo, or sometimes ivory, are divided into three categories: (1) honor tiles, (2) suit tiles, and (3) flower tiles. Mah Jong sets vary a bit in their honor and flower tile markings, but these are readily distinguishable. The following illustrations are typical of current sets available in the market:

1. The honor tiles consist of:
   A. Four green dragons (may depict the green Chinese character "fa" or a green-colored dragon design, and sometimes marked with the letter "F")

Four red dragons (may depict the red Chinese character "chung" or a red-colored dragon design, and sometimes marked with the letter "C")

Four white dragons (may be blank or bear a blue rectangular design, and may sometimes be marked with the letter "B" or "P")

A total of twelve tiles

B. Four east winds

Four south winds

Four west winds

Four north winds

A total of sixteen tiles

2. The suit tiles consist of three different suits of 36 tiles each, numbered from 1 through 9, four of each number, making a total of 108 tiles. The three suits are:

A. Bamboos (also called sticks, bams, or boos)

B. Circles (also called dots or balls)

C. Characters (also called cracks)

The suit tiles numbered 1 and 9 are called terminals, have higher point value, and are considered honors; the suit tiles numbered 2 through 8 are called simples and have less point value.

3. The flower tiles (sometimes called seasons) consist of two sets of four tiles each, numbered 1 through 4, with one set marked in one color, the other in another color. (Some Mah Jong sets, however, contain one set of eight different flower tiles.) Flower tiles are not used in actual play but represent a bonus to the holder, as will be explained in the discussion of the game.

Add together the 12 dragon tiles, the 16 wind tiles, the 108 suit tiles, and the 8 flower tiles, and the total is 144 basic tiles.

Some Mah Jong sets contain extra tiles known as the Cat, the Rat, the Cock, the Worm, the Old Man, and the Bag of Gold, and/or four joker tiles. These tiles do not enter into the formation of a Mah Jong hand but are used by players who enjoy the zest they add to the game. Their use is explained on pages 21–23.

There are usually several extra plain white tiles in most Mah Jong sets. These are used as replacement tiles and can be marked to match a lost tile.

Racks

The racks, while not essential, are helpful in that they hold the tiles at an easily visible angle and also provide holders for the chips or counters.

Counters

Modern Mah Jong sets sometimes come with poker chips or smaller round chips shaped like Chinese coins, with holes in the middle to facilitate stacking on rack prongs. Older sets or some Asian sets come with counting sticks of bone or plastic with denominations indicated by dots in various number and/or color formations.

In this manual, all limits and scoring are based on a 10,000-point stake that each player receives at the start of the game. Counters are divided into four denominations as follows:

Ten counters valued at	10 points each	100 points
Nine counters valued at	100 points each	900 points
Ten counters valued at	500 points each	5,000 points
Four counters valued at	1,000 points each	4,000 points
Total		10,000 points

Other variations of counter distribution may be made, if desired.

Before playing, stakes and limits to be paid should be determined. Counters too should be checked to assure accurate distribution. It is not necessary to put up money before beginning because, during the game, scores are settled through the exchange of counters.

If, however, a player loses all her counters during the game, she buys a new stake from any affluent player and, as a rule, pays cash to the seller.

Dice

A pair of dice is an essential accessory, as will be explained later.

Now that you beginners are familiar with your sets and accessories, let's play a game of Mah Jong.

Chapter 2
Preparation for the Game

New players are frequently confused and sometimes awed by the seemingly elaborate procedure necessary at the start of each hand of play. While there are several charming legendary reasons for this ritual, you will note, as you play, that it is an efficient method of organizing and distributing tiles, and it is simple to learn. It is similar to the shuffling and dealing of cards.

In Mah Jong there are no partners—each player is on his own and for himself. Once seated, the action starts.

Building the Wall

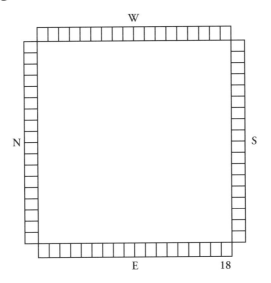

All tiles are placed on the table, facedown, and thoroughly shuffled by the players. Each player then draws tiles and builds a wall in front of his rack, two tiles high and eighteen tiles long—a total of thirty-six tiles. The four walls are then pushed together to form a square.

Winds

Before actual play starts it is essential to understand the meaning and use of winds.

There are four winds—East, South, West, and North—and each, in turn, is known as the wind of the round (synonymously, the prevailing wind). During its respective round, each wind is important from a scoring standpoint.

A *hand* of play is similar to a "deal" in bridge; players draw tiles and build hands by drawing and discarding until the hand is won, or until a draw results.

A *round* of play consists of a minimum of four hands, and a *game* consists of four rounds. As many games may be played as time and strength permit. The first round is always the East Wind round, the second the South Wind round, the third the West Wind round, and the fourth the North Wind round. Wind tiles serve to both indicate the rounds and identify the players. To start the game each player throws the dice, the highest becoming East Wind, a key position because it always opens the play and starts a new round. As will be explained later, East Wind pays or receives double. The game is played counterclockwise, which means the person to East's right is South Wind, the person opposite is West Wind, and the person to the left is North Wind.

Having won his title by his throw of the dice, East Wind retains this position as long as he wins up to seven times. When he loses, the East Wind title moves to the player on his right, and all other wind titles shift accordingly. After all four players have served in turn as East Wind, the next *round*, South round, starts, and the same procedure is repeated for this round. This is followed by the West Wind round, and finally by the North Wind round, which completes the first game. During each round, the player bearing the wind title of that specific round is known as *double* East, double South, or whatever the name of the round is. This has scoring advantages.

Opening the Wall

After the dice are rolled to determine the wind titles, East Wind throws the dice again to determine not only which wall is to be opened for drawing tiles but also *where* it is to be broken. Using the total shown on the dice, he counts in a counterclockwise direction, beginning with his own wall as number 1, South Wind as wall number 2, and so on. Therefore:

East Wind opens his own wall on a throw of 5 or 9.
South Wind opens his wall on a throw of 2 or 6 or 10.
West Wind opens his wall on a throw of 3 or 7 or 11.
North Wind opens his wall on a throw of 4 or 8 or 12.

East Wind then picks up the dice and places them on his rack for the duration of the hand—this is called "picking up your luck."

Once the wall to be opened has been determined, the player who built that wall proceeds to count the tiles from his *right-hand side* until he reaches the number thrown on the dice. In counting, the double layers of tiles are considered units of one. The player then lifts out these two tiles and places them facedown on top of the wall *to the right* of the break. This section of the wall is then known as the Garden (or Flower) Wall. The use of these tiles is explained later, but care should be taken that the top tile is placed to the right of the bottom tile.

Example: East Wind threw the dice for a total count of 8. North Wind breaks his wall at the eighth pair of tiles from *his* right-hand side. He lifts out this eighth pair of tiles and places them facedown, top tile on the right, on top of the wall to the right of the break.

East Wind begins the draw by taking the first four tiles from the opposite (left) side of the opening, known as the Open Wall, and places them on his rack. Each player in turn, in counterclockwise direction, takes the next four tiles from this wall, placing them on his rack, until each has twelve tiles. East Wind then takes the first and third top tiles from the Open Wall, and the other players each take one more tile from the end of the Open Wall. These are also placed on the respective racks. East Wind now has fourteen tiles in his hand, and the other players have thirteen. After the tiles are drawn from the Open Wall, players arrange them according to suit and decide what kind of hand or hands they will try to obtain.

The Open Wall should always be swung toward the center of the table so tiles are convenient to all four players. During the game it is the responsibility of each player to keep his section of the wall in easy reach of the other players. This is called "courtesy of the wall."

Flower Tiles

Next, the players declare their flower tiles by exposing them faceup on top of their racks. Tiles must be taken from the Garden Wall to replace exposed flower tiles. This is done in turn, starting with East Wind, in a counterclockwise direction.

If additional flower tiles are acquired when drawing from the Garden Wall, they too are exposed and replaced in the same manner. Please note that flower tiles *must* always be replaced to maintain a playing hand consisting of thirteen suit and honor tiles. Later in the game, if flower tiles are drawn, they are replaced in the same fashion.

Should a player draw four flower tiles, numbered 1 through 4 and *all* the same color, she has a "Flower Garden" and is immediately paid 1,000 points by each of the other players. These four flower tiles are then discarded and take no further part in the count of the hand.

Flower tiles are bonus tiles. They contribute to the hand in two ways: (1) they add points to the score but do not relate to its development into suits, and (2) they can provide doubles to the total count, as will be explained under "Scoring." Each flower tile relates to a wind and "prevails" during a round as follows:

No. 1 Flower Tile—East Wind
No. 2 Flower Tile—South Wind
No. 3 Flower Tile—West Wind
No. 4 Flower Tile—North Wind

Optional Tiles

If your set contains the extra tiles known as the Cat, the Rat, the Cock, and the Worm (shown above), or the Old Man and the Bag of Gold, the following rules apply:

1. These tiles may not be declared until actual play has started. They may be exposed at any expedient time when it is the player's turn. When exposed, they must be replaced by drawing from the Garden Wall.

2. These tiles may be passed to other players under the later-described procedures of the Charleston and the Ding Dong. (See page 30.)

3. In play the cat captures the rat if the rat has been exposed first; the cock captures the worm if the worm has been exposed first; and the old man captures the bag of gold if it has been exposed first. Obviously, if the cat, the cock, and the old man have been exposed, a player may safely declare the rat, the worm, or the bag of gold.

4. A player who is caught with any of these tiles *concealed* in his hand when a Mah Jong is declared has a scoreless hand.

5. These tiles, properly exposed, provide additional count and doubles for the possessor.

6. A player who *draws* (not captures) any four of these tiles is paid 1,000 points by each of the other players as a bonus. These tiles are then discarded and take no further part in the play of the hand.

If your set contains joker tiles, four of these may be used as "wild" tiles and may represent any tile a player needs for his hand. Use of more than four jokers is inadvisable, since this would unbalance the game. Once a joker tile has been used and declared, it cannot be replaced by the actual tile it represents. When four optional tiles are used, one two-tile stack is added to each of the East and West walls.

Beginners are advised to learn the basic game of Mah Jong before adopting these optional procedures.

Chapter 3
The Basic Game

The object of the basic game is to draw and discard tiles, in turn, to obtain a complete Mah Jong band of fourteen tiles consisting of four pungs (or kongs) and a pillow. A chow may be substituted for one pung. Exceptions are described in Chapter 5, "Special Hands."

Pung: **Three of a Kind**

There are two categories:

1. Exposed pung: This is obtained by having a pair of like tiles in the playing hand and claiming a third similar tile from any other player's discard as soon as the discard is made. Thereupon, the player announces "PUNG," picks up the tile, and, with the pair from her hand, places them faceup—exposed—on her rack. An unwanted tile is then discarded.

2. Concealed pung: This is obtained when a player, having a pair of like tiles in his playing hand, draws the third similar tile from the wall. He retains this pung in his hand and discards an unwanted tile. Concealed pungs (which have twice the value of exposed pungs) are placed upon the rack after Mah Jong has been announced, and the middle tile is turned facedown to indicate that it is a concealed pung.

Kong: Four of a Kind

There are two categories:

1. Exposed kong, which can be formed in either of two ways:

   A. When a player has a pung in her hand, she may pick up the fourth matching tile from any other player's discard as soon as it is made. Thereupon she announces "KONG" and places the four tiles faceup—exposed—on her rack. She draws a replacement tile from the Garden Wall, and it becomes a part of her playing hand. An unwanted tile is then discarded.

   B. When a player has an exposed pung on her rack and draws a fourth similar tile from the wall, she adds this fourth tile faceup on her rack to form a kong. She must draw a replacement tile from the Garden Wall, which becomes a part of her playing hand. An unwanted tile is discarded. However, a player may not claim the fourth tile from the discard to convert an exposed pung into a kong.

2. Concealed kong: This is formed when a player has a pung in his hand and draws the fourth matching tile from the wall. This concealed kong may be placed facedown on the player's rack, in which case a replacement tile must be drawn from the Garden Wall. If a player prefers not to declare the four matching tiles as a

concealed kong, he does not draw a replacement tile. In either case an unwanted tile is discarded.

As the game progresses, and a player shows her suit tiles on her rack, she turns up the two outside tiles of any concealed kongs on her rack to distinguish them from any exposed kongs she may have.

It is not necessary, or always expedient, to declare a kong the moment it is made. The player may retain the fourth tile concealed in his hand and, later in the game, declare it as a kong and at that time draw a replacement tile. This may be done at any time in the game when it is the player's turn. A player may prefer to utilize the fourth tile to form a chow, or to use it as two pairs in a special hand.

Please note: Kongs that have been declared on the rack, whether exposed or concealed, are always counted as a set of *three* (not four) tiles, and a replacement tile must be drawn to maintain the thirteen-tile playing hand. The fourth tile, to repeat, is not considered in the *count* of tiles but has value as a part of a kong. Kongs have high scoring value, they provide extra tiles, and hence, extra chances to improve hands, and if they are to count as *kongs*, they must be placed on the rack before the end of the game. If retained in the hand until a Mah Jong is declared, a kong is considered and counted as a pung.

Chow: A Sequence of Three Tiles in the Same Suit

This is formed when a player has two tiles in numerical order in the same suit in her hand and can complete a run or sequence by adding the third tile. However, the player can claim the required tile only from the discard of the person to her *immediate* left. The player announces "CHOW," declares the chow on her rack, and discards an unwanted tile. A player may also draw the third tile from the wall, in which case she retains the chow concealed in her hand and discards an unwanted tile.

Please note:

1. If a player is waiting for one tile to complete a chow to declare Mah Jong, she may chow that tile from any player in the game.

2. Chows have no score value and are used merely to complete a hand.

3. Only one chow is permitted in a completed Mah Jong hand (except in certain special hands that are described later).

Pillow: A Pair, or Two of a Kind

To Mah Jong, a hand must contain a pillow, in addition to the above-mentioned pungs, kongs, and/or chow. A player secures these two tiles by drawing from the walls, and these tiles are concealed in the hand. However, when a player needs only a single tile to complete his pillow and at the same time go Mah Jong, he may claim that tile from any other player's discard when it is made.

There are exceptions to this rule, as described in Chapter 5, "Special Hands."

Basic Hands

There are two basic hands that should be mastered before learning special hands. These are clean hands and pure hands.

Clean Hands

These are composed of four pungs (or kongs) of one suit and of honors (winds and dragons) plus a pillow of the same suit or of honor tiles. If desired, a chow in the same suit may be substituted for one pung or kong.

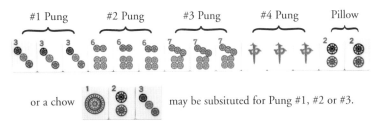

or a chow may be subsituted for Pung #1, #2 or #3.

Pure Hands

These are composed of four pungs (or kongs) plus a pair of the same suit with no honors. If desired, one chow may be substituted for one pung or kong. This hand, harder to achieve, has a higher scoring value than a clean hand.

Many Western players require that, except as noted in Chapter 5, "Special Hands," a basic Mah Jong hand must not contain tiles of more than one suit.

When a player has achieved either a clean hand or a pure hand with the specified four sets of pungs (or kongs) and a pair (or one chow as set forth above), he goes Mah Jong.

Playing the Game

The play often begins with the popular optional procedures listed below:

Charleston (or Razzle): An Optional Procedure

After the tiles are drawn and flowers declared, each player exchanges three tiles, facedown, with the person opposite him; next, East Wind and West Wind exchange three tiles, facedown, with the players on their right; and finally, East Wind and West Wind exchange three tiles, facedown, with the players on their left. Each player thus has the same number of tiles that he drew from the wall and, hopefully, a better hand plus an idea of what the other players are doing. Many Western players use the Charleston only during a *goulash* (a replayed hand after a dead hand).

Ding Dong: An Optional Procedure

When the Charleston has been accepted as part of the game, at *the option of East* a further exchange of tiles may be made. Each player may pass one tile, facedown, to each of the other players. This procedure may be repeated up to three times—if East Wind wishes.

The Kitty (or Goolie): An Optional Procedure

Players often agree to pool a predetermined sum of money before the play begins. A 100-point counter each is the usual amount. Known as the "kitty," the pool is won by the player who Mah Jongs on a complete pung (or kong) hand (no chows). The kitty must be claimed before the Mah Jong hand is discarded, or it is forfeited.

Whenever the winning hand does not qualify for the kitty, each player adds another 100-point counter. This pool makes for a more exciting game since a sizeable amount can accumulate quickly. At the beginning of the hand, if double dice are thrown, each player adds an additional 100-point counter to the kitty.

By this time, players have decided what kind of hands they will try to develop, and they try to achieve these, as said before, by drawing and discarding tiles. East Wind begins the actual play by discarding a tile, announcing it by name, and placing it faceup on the table, thus reducing his tile count to thirteen. This tile may be claimed by any other player, to form a pung or kong. Only South Wind may claim it for a chow.

If the discarded tile is not claimed, it becomes a dead tile, and South Wind draws a tile from the Open Wall and discards an unwanted tile, always remembering to name the discard. West Wind follows this procedure, and then North Wind, and so on. Whenever a tile drawn from the wall is retained in the player's hand, an unwanted tile must be discarded.

This drawing and discarding is repeated in a counterclockwise fashion until one player claims a tile for a pung, kong, or chow. Any player may claim a discard for a pung or kong at any time, regardless of whether or not he is next in turn. After he has completed his play, declared it on his rack, and discarded, the hand is resumed by the next player to his right.

Note that, from time to time, a player may miss a turn. For example, if East discards a Green Dragon and West pungs it, South misses his turn because the game will be continued, after West's discard, by North's drawing a tile.

Discards

A discard may be claimed only if it can be exposed at once faceup on the rack as part of a pung, kong, or chow.

A discarded tile must be claimed before the next player picks and racks or discards, or it becomes a dead tile and cannot be claimed during the hand. Players should watch all discards carefully, or they may find they are waiting for a dead tile.

If more than one player claims the same discarded tile, the procedure is as follows:

1. The player who can Mah Jong on that tile has priority.
2. The player next in turn to the discarder has precedence if more than one player claims the tile for Mah Jong.
3. The player who requires the tile to complete a pung has precedence, regardless of his position, over the player who needs it to complete a chow.

Going Mah Jong

When a player has completed her hand, she announces Mah Jong, places all her tiles faceup on her rack, and counts her score. A Mah Jong hand must contain a playing count of fourteen tiles. This means the tile drawn to complete the hand is not discarded.

A player may go Mah Jong on either (1) an exposed or (2) a concealed hand.

1. An *exposed hand* means that tiles have been exposed on the rack, and that all tiles have been drawn from the discards or from the walls.

2. A *concealed hand* means that no tiles have been exposed on the rack and that all tiles have been drawn from the walls with the exception of the last, or Mah Jong, tile that may be taken from either the wall or the discard.

If the tile that enables a player to go Mah Jong is drawn from the Open Wall, it is considered "concealed," and so is the pung it completes.

The player who Mah Jongs is always paid first, is paid by the other players, and does not pay them for their hands regardless of score. Other players expose their uncompleted hands on their racks in counterclockwise order from the winner's position, determine their scores, and settle their differences by exchange of counters.

It sometimes happens, during the drawing and discarding of tiles, that the end of the wall is approached. When this occurs, the loose tiles on top of the wall are replaced in their original positions and drawn as regular tiles until the wall has no tiles remaining. (See Dead Hands, page 43.)

Tiles are now thrown into the center of the table, shuffled, and the walls rebuilt for the next hand.

You have now played a hand of Mah Jong. The next step is to learn how to score your hand. Knowledge of scoring is important from a playing standpoint: it enables you to evaluate your hand, to decide on the wisest course of play, and to try for higher scores.

So, on to a study of scoring, which you will find surprisingly simple.

Chapter 4
Scoring, Penalties, and Variations

In this manual, a hand with a score of 500 or more points is considered a limit hand, and, to avoid paying tremendous sums, a payment limit of 500 points is also set. It is standard practice that East Wind pays or receives double.

There are hands that always receive limit payments although their actual count is below 500 points. These are special hands and are listed in Chapter 5. When double dice are thrown, all payments are doubled. As stated before, the player who goes Mah Jong is always the first to count her hand according to the point value of pungs, kongs, flowers, and so on, as listed below, to arrive at her basic score. If this is not a multiple of ten, she converts her basic score to the next highest unit of ten and, as a bonus for going Mah Jong, adds twenty points to the total. This figure, her total count, is then doubled for each double contained in her hand, and she is paid in full or up to the limit by the other players.

The other players determine their scores in the same manner (except they do not receive a Mah Jong bonus). By subtracting lower scores from higher scores, players arrive at their net scores and settle their differences by exchanging counters up to the stated limit. If scores are identical, they "wash"—no payment is made.

If double dice are thrown, scores, and hence payments, are doubled, and as said before, East Wind always pays or receives double.

A simple way to settle scores is to use numbered suit tiles to indicate individual scores and subtract lesser from greater:

South Score	480	4 萬	8 circles
West Score	120	1 circle	2 bamboo
South receives from West	360	3 circles	6 bamboo

If the difference between scores exceeds 500, the limit (500) is paid, East paying or receiving double.

Scoring is not complicated. Two factors are involved: *counting* the hand and *doubling* the total count. It is important to count accurately because, once payment is made, errors cannot be corrected.

Counting

Flower tiles and optional tiles count four points each.

Pungs

	Exposed	Concealed
Suit tiles 2s through 8s	2 points	4 points
Suit tiles 1s and 9s	4 points	8 points
Winds and dragons	4 points	8 points

Kongs

	Exposed	Concealed
Suit tiles 2s through 8s	8 points	16 points
Suit tiles 1s and 9s	16 points	32 points
Winds and dragons	16 points	32 points

Chows have no score value except as in number 3 below.

Two Points are scored for:
1. A pair of terminals (1s or 9s)
2. A pair of honors (winds and dragons)
3. Punging or konging the first tile discarded by East Wind. This is known as a "sweep." One tile is turned sideways on the player's rack to serve as a reminder that two points are to be added to the value of this pung or kong.
4. If a chow is formed by the first tile discarded by East, this is also considered a sweep and has a scoring value of two points.

For going Mah Jong, twenty points is added to basic score.

Doubling

Clean hand (all *one* suit with winds and/or dragons)	one double
Pure hand (one suit—no honors)	three doubles
Each of the flowers of the round	one double
Each pung or kong of dragons	one double
Pung or kong of the player's own wind	one double
Pung or kong of the wind of the round	one double
Each of the players' own flowers	one double
Concealed Mah Jong hand	one double

Drawing Mah Jong tile from Garden Wall   one double

Optional tiles: cat, rat, cock, worm, old man,

    and bag of gold—each   one double

Note: Score is doubled once if a player holds his own flower, once again for his own wind, and once again if the flower and/or wind "prevails." Score is optionally doubled if both dice showed the same number when opening the wall ("double dice").

        A pure hand (three doubles) is often referred to as an "eight times" hand because a quick way to arrive at the score is to multiply the total count by eight.

        Scoring for special hands is listed in Chapter 5 along with the descriptions of the hands.

Examples of Scoring

1. West Wind Mah Jongs on South Wind round with the following hand.

COUNT	POINTS
His own flower—No. 3	4
A concealed Pung—eight characters	4
An exposed kong—nine characters	16
An exposed kong—white dragons	16
An exposed pung—south winds	4
A pair—west winds	2
His basic score is:	46

Basic score is converted to next highest unit of 10.

46 goes to	50
Mah Jong bonus	20
Total count	70

DOUBLES:

One double for clean hand	70 x 2 = 140
One double for his own flower	140 x 2 = 280
One double for kong of dragons	280 x 2 = 560
One double for pung of prevailing wind	560 x 2 = 1,120

Any hand with a score of 500 points or more is considered a limit hand. Therefore, West Wind receives payment of 500 from South and North, and East Wind pays double, or 1,000.

Had double dice been thrown, West would have received payment of 1,000 from South and North, while East Wind would have paid double, or 2,000.

2. West Wind with the hand described above is unable to secure the second West Wind tile before North Wind completes his Mah Jong hand. In this case his score is:

COUNT	POINTS
His own flower—No. 3	4
A concealed Pung—eight characters	4
An exposed kong—nine characters	16
An exposed kong—white dragons	16
An exposed pung—south winds	4
One west wind tile	no count
His basic score is:	44

Basic score is converted to next highest unit of 10:

44 goes to	50
Total count	50

DOUBLES:

One double for clean hand	50 x 2 = 100
One double for his own flower	100 x 2 = 200
One double for kong of dragons	200 x 2 = 400
One double for pung of prevailing wind	400 x 2 = 800

Total score is over 500, a limit hand. West Wind receives 500 points from South and 1,000 points from East.

3. East Wind Mah Jongs with a pure hand (one suit only—no winds or dragons) in the East Wind round. This is the hand he holds:

COUNT	POINTS
His own flower—No. 1	4
No. 3 flower	4
An exposed kong—one bamboo	16
An exposed pung—four bamboos	2
A concealed kong—eight bamboos	16
An exposed pung—nine bamboos	4
A pair—two bamboos	0
His basic score is:	46

Basic score is converted to next highest unit of 10:

46 goes to	50
Mah Jong bonus	20
Total count	70

DOUBLES:

Three doubles for pure hand	70 x 8 = 560
Two doubles for his own flower, which is also the prevailing flower	560 x 2 x 2 = 2,240

A score of 2,240 is well over the limit, so East is paid the limit. In the case of East, this is always double, or 1,000.

4. There are many low-scoring hands, as is evidenced by this example: South Wind Mah Jongs on East Wind round with two pungs, one kong, one chow, and a pillow, a pure hand (all bamboos).

COUNT	POINTS
An exposed pung—nine bamboos	4
An exposed pung—six bamboos	2
An exposed kong—three bamboos	8
An exposed pair—one bamboo	2
An exposed chow—7-8-9 bamboos	0
His basic score is:	16

Basic score is converted to next highest unit of 10:

16 goes to	20
Mah Jong bonus	20
Total count	40

DOUBLES:

Three doubles for pure hand (multiply by 8)   40 x 8 = 320

East pays double—640—and the other players pay 320.

As stated before, a limit is always paid on any hand with points over 500. When two or more players (other than the player who Mah Jongs) have limit hands, and a player subtracts her score from another player's with the net result of more than 500, she pays only the limit—with East always paying (or receiving) double.

Confusion in payment of scores frequently arises when double dice are thrown. The total score is doubled for payment, but a player never receives more than double the 500 limit, or 1,000; East pays or receives 2,000.

For example: South Mah Jongs on double dice with a total score of 960—a limit hand. East pays him 2,000; the other players pay him 1,000.

East Wind Mah Jongs on double dice with a score of 180. He is paid 720 by each player because:

180 doubled once (because he is East) = 360

360 doubled (for double dice)   = 720

Settling Stakes

At the end of the Mah Jong session, the players settle the original 10,000-point stake as follows:

Each player counts his counters to the nearest 100.

Each player puts all "odd lots" (ten-point counters totaling less than 100 points) in a common pool. Dice are tossed for these counters, and the highest cast adds them to his counters.

Each player totals his counters and calculates the difference between what he holds and his original 10,000-point stake. Players place numbered tiles on their racks to indicate their standing.

Total winnings will match total losses. Losers pay cash value based on the predetermined stake value.

Dead Hands

When all tiles have been drawn from the wall, and no player has been able to go Mah Jong, a dead hand is declared:

No scores are counted.

Tiles are reshuffled.

The wall is rebuilt.

An additional contribution is made to the kitty.

Same East player rolls the dice again to open the wall (the dice do not pass to the next player) for one hand only. This replayed hand is called a *goulash*. It is customary to precede the goulash with a Charleston.

Penalties

All games have penalties, and this is true in Mah Jong:

1. If a player discovers he has too few tiles in his hand, he is not permitted to correct the error, and therefore he cannot Mah Jong. However, he may count his hand but is not entitled to doubles for (a) a clean hand, (b) a pure hand, or (c) any of the honor hands, because the missing tile or tiles might alter his hand.

2. If a player discovers he has too many tiles in his hand, he is not permitted to correct the error. He cannot Mah Jong, has a scoreless hand, and must pay the other players their hand values.

3. If a player declares Mah Jong in error (whether or not his hand is exposed) and any other player exposes his hand, the game cannot continue. The erring player must pay a limit to the others. However, if no hands are exposed, the play may continue.

4. If a player fails to declare a flower tile by the time a Mah Jong is declared, his hand automatically contains too few tiles and is treated as number 1 above. In addition he is not permitted to count the undeclared flower tile. Care should be taken not to confuse the number 1 bamboo tiles with the flower tiles.

5. If a player has an undeclared kong in his hand when Mah Jong is announced, it is counted as a pung.

6. Optionally, if joker tiles are used, a player who has one or more of these in his hand when Mah Jong is announced has a scoreless hand.

Two-Handed Mah Jong

Two-handed Mah Jong is similar to the four-handed game. A two-handed game is useful to beginners in learning the tiles and the development of hands. However, in playing there are some differences: the players sit opposite each other and are always East Wind and West

Wind. They cannot go Mah Jong unless the hand contains four or more doubles, and no chows are permitted. Scoring is the same, but the players pay each other. This is the only time the player who Mah Jongs pays the difference in his score.

Three-Handed Mah Jong

The same procedures exist as in the four-handed game: four walls are built, tiles drawn, and suits arranged. There is, of course, always a *vacant* wind position. If the optional procedure of the Charleston is used, the final exchange of tiles is made with the wall. Scoring is the same.

Chapter 5
Special Hands

Originally, Mah Jong was played without special hands, and there are still many who prefer this game. At the other extreme are those who play only special hands. And here is where the arguments start—the purists will object, the open-minded cheer. You must decide what system you wish to follow, and if you include special hands in your game, all players must agree on which hands are acceptable. Most players feel that the more hands they master, the greater their chances of success. Completed special hands are paid the stated limits, East being paid double, and double dice doubling payments. Uncompleted special hands are treated and counted in the same manner as regular hands (see Counting, pages 36–37).

Pair Hands

In pair hands, a kong is considered as two pairs but must be concealed *in the hand.*

1. Dirty Pairs: concealed—half limit
   Seven pairs of anything.

2. Clean Pairs: concealed—half limit
   Seven pairs in *one suit* with pairs of winds or dragons.

3. Heavenly Twins (Doublets): concealed—limit
   Seven pairs in one suit only—no winds or dragons.
4. Honor Pairs (All Pair Honor Hand): concealed—half limit
   Seven pairs of terminals (1s and 9s) and/or honors.
5. Knitting: concealed—half limit
   Combination of seven pairs in any two matched suits. A paired combination of circles and bamboos, circles and characters, or bamboos and characters. No winds or dragons.

6. Windfall: concealed—half limit
   Five pairs of one suit plus one of each wind.

7. Dragon's Breath: concealed—limit
   Five pairs of one suit, and one of each dragon, with one dragon paired.
8. Dragonet: concealed—limit
   Three pairs of one suit plus any honor paired, and six odd honors. No terminals may be used.

9. Gertie's Garter: concealed—limit
   1 through 7 in two suits. (See Knitting.)

10. Crochet (Triple Knitting): concealed—half limit
    Four sets of tiles and pair—each set of three must have one of
    the same numbered tile in each suit. The pair must be a knitted
    pair.

Sequence Hands

11. News Hand (Wriggling Snake): concealed—limit
    1 through 9 in one suit plus one of each wind, with one of these
    winds or terminals paired.

12. Dragon's Tail (Honor Line-Up): concealed—limit
    1 through 9 in one suit plus either a pung of winds and a pair
    of dragons, or a pung of dragons and a pair of winds.

13. Nine United Sons (Heavenly Gates or Gates of Heaven):
    concealed—double limit
    All one suit as follows: 2 through 8, three of each terminal, with
    any one of these simples paired.

14. Five Odd Honors: concealed—limit
    1 through 9 in one suit plus five odd winds and dragons. This
    hand does not contain a pair.
15. Run, Pung, and a Pair: concealed—limit
    1 through 9 in one suit plus a pung in the same suit and a pair
    in the same suit.

16. Seven Up (Greta's Garden): concealed—limit
    1 through 7 in one suit plus one of each wind and one each of
    dragon. This hand does not contain a pair.

Jewel Hands

17. Jade Hand: exposed—limit
    Pungs or kongs of the green bamboo tiles (2s, 3s, 4s, 6s, or 8s),
    with any one of these tiles paired.
18. All Pair Jade Hand: concealed—limit
    Seven pairs of green bamboo and/or the green dragon tiles. The
    kong that is needed to form this hand is considered as two pairs.
19. Imperial Jade Hand: exposed—double limit
    Pungs or kongs of green bamboo and green dragon tiles plus a
    pair of any one of these tiles.
20. Ruby Jade Hand: exposed—limit
    A pung or kong of red dragons, a pung or kong of green dragons,
    a pung or kong of red bamboos (1s, 5s, 7s, or 9s), a pung or
    kong of green bamboos (2s, 3s, 4s, 6s, or 8s), one of the red or
    green bamboos paired.

21. All Pair Ruby Hand: concealed—limit
Seven pairs of red bamboos (1s, 5s, 7s, or 9s) and/or the red dragon tiles. The kongs that are necessary to form this hand are considered as pairs.

22. Imperial Ruby Hand: exposed—double limit
Pungs or kongs of red bamboos (1s, 5s, 7s, or 9s) or red dragon tiles, plus a pair of any of these tiles.

23. Ruby Crack Hand: exposed—limit
Pungs or kongs and a pair in characters (2s, 3s, 4s, 6s, or 8s) and/or the red dragon tiles.

24. Pearl Hand: exposed—limit
Pungs or kongs and a pair in circles (2s, 3s, 4s, or 8s) and/or the white dragon tiles.

Honor Hands

25. All Honor Hand: exposed—limit
Pungs or kongs of 1s and/or 9s in any suit with pungs of winds and/or dragons and a pair of any of the honors.

26. Heads and Tails (Ones and Nines): exposed—limit
Pungs or kongs of 1s and 9s in any suit plus a pair of either 1s or 9s—no winds or dragons.

27. Unique Wonders (Thirteen Impossible): concealed—double limit

One of each wind, one of each dragon, one of each 1 and 9 in each suit, plus an additional one of any of these tiles.

28. Windy Dragons: concealed—double limit

Two pungs (not kongs) of any dragons and one pair of each of the winds.

29. Three Great Scholars: exposed—limit

Pungs or kongs of the three dragons plus a pung or a kong or a chow in one suit and a pair in that suit or a pair of winds.

30. The Four Blessings: exposed—double limit

Pungs or kongs of the four winds plus a pair of anything.

31. Gone with the Wind: exposed—double limit

Pungs or kongs of the four winds and one pair of dragons.

32. Windy Chows: concealed—half limit

One chow of characters, one chow of circles, one chow of bamboo plus one of each of the winds, with any one of these winds paired.

33. Hachi-Ban: concealed—limit

A sequence of eight in a suit with three pairs of winds or three pairs of dragons.

Gates Hands

34. Confused Gates: concealed—limit

    A pung of 1s in one suit, a pung of 9s in a second suit, and a sequence of 2 through 8 in a third suit, with any one of these simples paired.

35. True Gates: concealed—limit

    One suit only: a pung of 1s, a pung of 9s, plus a pair of the 2s, 4s, 6s, and 8s.

36. Dragon Gates: concealed—limit

    The suit must be used with its corresponding dragon. A pung of 1s or of 9s, a pung of corresponding dragons plus a sequence of 2 through 8, with any one of these simples paired. Red dragons are used with characters, white dragons with circles, and green dragons with bamboos.

37. Golden Gate: concealed—limit

    The suit must be used with its corresponding dragon. A pung of 1s or of 9s, with pairs of 2s, 4s, 6s, and 8s, plus a pung of corresponding dragons. Red dragons are used with characters, white dragons with circles, and green dragons with bamboos.

Numbers Hands

38. Up You Go: concealed—double limit

    2, 44, 666, 8888 in one suit with NEWS (for example, one of each of the four wind tiles). The kong of 8s must be concealed.

39. Down You Go: concealed—double limit

    2222, 444, 66, 8 in one suit with NEWS. The kong of 2s must be concealed.

40. Chop Suey: concealed—limit

    1-2-3 in each suit with NEWS and any one of these winds paired.

41. Chow Mein: concealed—limit

    7-8-9 in each suit with NEWS and any one of these winds paired.

42. Civil War: concealed—double limit

    1, 8, 6, 1 in one suit and 1, 8, 6, 5 in a second suit plus a pung of north winds, and a pung of south winds.

43. Numbers Racket (Parallel Hand): exposed—double limit

    Pungs of the same number in three suits plus either a pung and a pair of winds or a pung and a pair of dragons. No terminals.

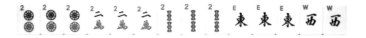

44. Double Numbers: exposed—double limit

    Two pungs of the same numbers in two different suits plus a pair of winds or dragons. No terminals.

45. Triple East: exposed—double limit

    Three different pungs in different suits and a pung of east winds plus a pair of red dragons. No terminals.

46. Triple South: exposed—double limit

    Three different pungs in different suits and a pung of south winds plus a pair of green dragons. No terminals.

Odds and Ends

47. Christmas Cheer: exposed—double limit

    A pung of 2s and a pung of 5s in the same suit and a pung of red dragons plus a pung of green dragons and a pair of white dragons.

48. Christmas Eve: exposed—double limit

    A pung of red bamboos (1s, 5s, 7s, or 9s), a pung of green bamboos (2s, 3s, 4s, 6s, or 8s), a pung of red dragons, a pung of green dragons, and a pair of white dragons.

49. All Kong Hand: exposed—limit

    Four kongs in one suit and/or in winds or dragons plus a pair of the suit or honor tiles.

Two unusual situations that sometimes occur are:

A. Heaven's Grace: double limit

   This is a long shot and is also called The Going Out of the Gods. East Wind Mah Jongs with his original fourteen tiles.

B. Earth's Grace: limit

   This is scored when a player completes his Mah Jong on the first discard made by East Wind. The player receives a limit regardless of the actual scoring points in his hand.

There are other special hands, some deriving from those described above, some quite different. Those included are the better known and more popular ones.

Chapter 6
Strategy

Mah Jong is a fascinating game of both strategy and luck. You have no control over what tiles you pick—that's where the luck comes in. Strategy must be used in choosing what to discard, and in the timing of those discard choices.

Basic Strategy

The best beginner strategy is to go for basic clean or pure hands, and to collect valuable honor sets when possible.

Remember that chows are the easiest sets to make, and that these rules permit no more than one chow in a basic hand. So do not be in a hurry to make a chow.

Know your seat wind and the round wind. Pungs of the right winds add to the score when you can make them.

Advanced Strategy

Advanced strategy includes principles to consider when discarding or claiming others' discards, as well as for choosing which hands to build and which sets to collect. In addition, the strategy can vary depending on how far the game has progressed.

A hand of Mah Jong normally consists of three phases. Each phase is approximately seven to eight turns. The first phase moves rapidly as the players concentrate on building their hands (sometimes pursuing multiple options). In the second phase, players are making decisions (discarding their secondary possibilities). The turns of the third phase are crucial because it's highly likely that someone is going to win now. After the deal, mentally divide the wall into thirds as an aid to determining the phases. Throughout the hand, keep an eye on the wall—as it gets shorter, increase your wariness.

Phase One—Build, Collect (first seven to eight turns)

Evaluate. First, evaluate the hand for possibilities of special hands. If you have eight or more tiles toward a special hand, you should go for it. It only takes a few big scoring hands to make you the overall winner for the evening. Usually, though, you'll just work toward a basic one-suit hand.

Discarding. Choose some initial discards. It's normal to discard single honor tiles early on (as this prevents others from punging them).

Try to remember who discarded what. Determine what suits the player at your left and right are keeping. Don't hold out for the same suit as the player at your left (he won't give you any), and don't discard the suit wanted by the player at your right (she'll surely take them). Throw the suit wanted by players across and left (they can't chow them).

Shaping. In the first phase, it is normal to build toward multiple options. Cull tiles that don't advance the hand. Collecting tiles serendipitously, one or more options take shape. Be prepared to change your plan depending on your picks and the discards of others.

Calling. Don't leap hastily to take every discard that you can. A pair in the hand is often worth more than a pung in the melds. Once you make an exposure, your options are reduced.

Completed sets in the hand need not be exposed. Concealment is doubly advantageous. Concealed sets score more points, and other people can only guess at what you have hidden in your hand.

Kongs are more valuable than pungs, but if you have the chance to call for a kong, consider keeping the concealed pung instead. A picked fourth tile could be used in a chow, and you can always add to the pung anytime.

Phase Two—Choose, Attack (middle seven to eight turns)

Choosing. If the hand has a couple of options, it's necessary to choose and pursue one of them once the hand is in the middle phase. If the hand has begun to take shape in one particular direction, choose to pursue that direction.

Discarding. Do not continue to hold potentially dangerous discards beyond phase two. Dangerous tiles are better thrown early, not late. Terminals and honors are, generally speaking, safe to discard early in the game and dangerous to throw later. Middle simples (3–7) are the most dangerous to discard later in the game.

Regardless of this general principle, though, you should also consider the tiles you can see. Discards and exposures can reveal a lot about what tiles are dangerous or safe to throw.

Calling. An incomplete chow that can be filled at both ends doubles your chances. If you're holding a 4–6 combination (needing a 5 in the middle) and you pick a 3, then you should discard the 6 so you have a two-way call.

If you have a clear direction for the hand, and a tile is discarded that helps you move the hand toward completion, then by all means call it.

Sometimes, though, you *can* call a tile that does *not* progress the hand.

For example, if you are holding 1, 2, 3 and someone discards a 4, there is no advantage in calling and exposing the chow. You already had a chow, fully concealed in the hand, and now you have an exposed chow (which gives other players information about what you are doing).

Phase Three—Defend, Hold

Safe Discards. Sometimes it's wise to break up the hand to keep from giving somebody else the win. "Dogging" (throwing away safe tiles that your hand needs) is a valid defensive strategy when your chances of winning are low; this will allow you to achieve a draw.

On the other hand, nobody's hands are scored in a draw game. If you are holding valuable scoring sets or patterns, sometimes it can be better to give someone a win so that you can score points from the other nonwinners.